TX 2047 $2.45

INFORMAL SCHOOLS
IN BRITAIN TODAY

Trends
in School
Design

Eric Pearson

Trends in School Design

Eric Pearson

Citation Press, New York 1972

© Schools Council Publications 1972.

ISBN 590-09521-8

Library of Congress Catalog Card number 76-16888

Cover photograph by courtesy of Henry Grant

This book is published simultaneously in Great
Britain, Canada and other countries of the British
Commonwealth by Macmillan Education Ltd and
in the United States by Citation Press, Library
and Trade Division Scholastic Magazines, Inc.

Designer Richard Hollis

Printed in the U.S.A.

Preface

The purpose of the Anglo-American Primary Education Project is to provide descriptions of the way that British primary schools work. They are published in this series of booklets under the general title of *British Primary Schools Today* and they have been written for American and British educators and teachers-in-training as well as for the general public.

The authors are either practitioners or expert observers of British primary education and, in most cases, they document the work of the schools through detailed case examples; where it is relevant, implications are stated and conclusions drawn. It is not the intention to provide theoretical discussions or prescriptive manuals to informal education, but rather to present accounts from which deductions and generalizations can be made. In so doing, these booklets draw on the experience of that large minority of primary schools that have adopted informal methods.

It is hoped that the booklets will help educators who are looking for examples to substantiate change in particular schools and also those who are concerned, as teachers, educators or administrators, with the wider implications of the education of young children. For students who plan to become teachers these accounts of what happens in the classrooms of British primary schools provide ample material for discussion as well as helpful insights into the practice of teaching.

The series has been prepared under the aegis of the Schools Council in England with the support of the Ford Foundation in the United States. Planning was assisted by a small Anglo-American advisory group whose members are listed on page 4. The views expressed are however personal to each author.

British Directorate

Geoffrey Cockerill, Project Chairman/Joint Secretary, Schools Council for Curriculum and Examinations, London.

John Blackie/Formerly Chief Inspector, Primary Education, Department of Education and Science, London.

Molly Brealey/Formerly Principal, Froebel Institute College of Education, London.

Maurice Kogan, Project Co-ordinator/Professor of Government and Social Administration, School of Social Sciences, Brunel University, Uxbridge, Middlesex.

American Participants

J. Myron Atkin/Dean, School of Education, University of Illinois, Urbana, Illinois.

Ann Cook/Co-director, Community Resources Institute, 270 W. 96th Street, New York.

Joseph Featherstone/Writer; Lecturer, John Fitzgerald Kennedy School of Government, Institute of Politics, Harvard University, Cambridge, Massachusetts.

Professor David Hawkins/Director, Mountain View Center for Environmental Education, University of Colorado, Boulder, Colorado.

Herb Mack/Co-director, Community Resources Institute, 270 W. 96th Street, New York.

Marjorie Martus/Program Officer, The Ford Foundation, New York, N.Y.

Casey Murrow/Teacher, Wilmington Elementary School, Wilmington, Vermont.

Liza Murrow/Antioch-Putney Graduate School of Education, Putney, Vermont.

Mary Lela Sherburne/Director, Pilot Communities Project, Education Development Center, Newton, Mass.

Contents

Acknowledgements

Sources of material for this booklet have been many, but the author is especially indebted to Miss Edith Moorhouse for the invaluable help she has given throughout, and to the Architects and Buildings Branch of the Department of Education and Science for its cooperation and criticism. Special thanks are also due to officers of the Inner London Education Authority, the Oxfordshire and Nottinghamshire County Councils and the Secretary of the Salford Roman Catholic Schools Commission for their help and advice.

Acknowledgement is given to the following for permission to reproduce plans of schools:

The controller of Her Majesty's Stationery Office, for Finmere Primary School and the Eveline Lowe Primary School;

The County Architect for Oxfordshire, for Eynsham Primary School, and Brize Norton Primary School;

The County Architect for Nottinghamshire for the Frederick Harrison Infants' School, Stapleford;

The Ellis/Williams Partnership, Manchester, for St Thomas of Canterbury RC Primary School, Manchester;

Cassidy, Farrington and Dennys Partnership, for Compton Primary School, London.

The photographs are reproduced with the permission of the following:

Her Majesty's Stationery Office (pages 42, 47)

Layland Ross Limited (bottom, page 74)

Allan Hurst (pages 58, 60, 74)

A & C Black (pages 33, 37)

The Author

Eric Pearson was a schoolmaster until 1939, when he was headmaster of a large senior boys' school. In that year he joined the inspectorate of the then Board of Education and worked with it continuously until his retirement in 1968. For seventeen years he served in the Architects Branch at the Ministry of Education in London, and was engaged in research and development work concerned with educational requirements for all types of school building. Prior to his retirement he was HM Inspector nationally responsible for this work.

He is school-building consultant to the OECD and assists with their work in developing countries. He has also acted as co-ordinator and rapporteur of the Council of Europe's work on the educational aspects of school building.

More recently he has been working with schools of architecture in the UK.

Introduction

This booklet concerns the physical and human environment created for the learning of young children. The design problem, stated simply, is to produce a harmonious whole. A school building should be set within its natural landscape in such a way that the inter-relation of outside and inside offers the children an almost unlimited range of educational opportunity. Such a physical coherence reflects the current view that the whole environment educates.

Primary schools in England and Wales tend to be smaller than in many other countries, even in the densely populated towns and cities. In the rural areas there are still some 6,000 schools of up to four classes with less than a hundred pupils on roll. Very few new village schools have been built in the postwar years, new schools having been required most of all in growing urban areas. On both social and educational grounds, it has been considered important that young children should be able to identify themselves personally with the school communities to which they belong, and for this reason these have been kept small. Of new schools built in urban and suburban areas, the seven-class all-through primary school with a maximum of 280 pupils is the most common size. Where there is a two-class entry of children each year, resulting in a school of 560 children, it is customary to divide it into separate infant (six classes) and junior (eight classes) departments. Some schools for as many as 560 pupils have been built but, on the whole, local education authorities do not favour primary schools larger than this.

To an outsider, the working organization of a British primary school or class may appear unformulated and therefore incomprehensible. In this country, the law does not lay down what kinds of schools shall be built, what the teachers shall teach or how they shall teach it. British schools tend to let matters of this kind work themselves out in the light of experience and experiment. Teachers in charge, together with their staffs, while working within broadly accepted professional standards, determine for themselves the framework of the organization and the content of the curriculum. In the most successful schools, staff meet regularly to discuss objectives, methods and standards, modifying them as occasion demands. British primary school teachers enjoy a great measure of freedom. They accept the responsibility it throws upon them, and many of them exercise the initiative it gives them. This freedom enables those who use it to break through the frontiers of conventional practice to experiment in new fields of learning. It allows them to respond to change whether this be in social attitudes or technological advance.

What sort of a design brief can there be for a school which may frequently change its organization and methods? Is there a continuous thread of principle or philosophy which might provide a basis for design? There is a school of thought among both educators and architects which believes that press button moving walls are the answer. But this view has not sufficient regard for the nature and purpose of the school environment. In education, people respond to the character of an environment designed for its particular learning function; it can promote or even hinder the process. Even in very old buildings, some spaces adapted to new teaching methods by ingenious, sensitive teachers are models, not only of smooth working efficiency, but also in the subtlety of their exposure of the children to varying light, colour and textures, and to many 'things' which excite curiosity and promote thought. Through all these, the teacher is able to speak to the children far more clearly than by any exposition she can offer. The approach to the most successful school design in this country is through the inspiration and practice of such teachers. Some of them work in obscure places, but, wherever they are to be found, architects should be there, observing the arrangements made, discussing them with the teachers, and studying the response of the children. These represent the frontier of advance for primary school design from which further progress might be made.

The first part of this booklet discusses briefly the significant changes in social attitudes and educational practice from which new ideas about primary school design have emerged during the last twenty years. Equally significant has been the change in attitudes of architects and administrators whose concern has been to design schools to match the new educational concepts and to provide them at a cost which the country could afford. The second part deals with primary school design as an evolving process during the same period.

1 Influences on Primary School Buildings

Changes in social attitudes and education practice

Recent reports of the Central Advisory Council for Education in England[1] have revealed a growing awareness of the importance to the individual of his family, his social background, and the neighbourhood in which he is brought up. Learning is the continual process of interaction between the learner and his physical and human environment, and social deprivation may have serious consequences for a child. Full employment, the rise in incomes, better housing, the easy acquisition of labour-saving household equipment, and the development of the health and social services in recent years, have brought about a great improvement in parental circumstances. The growing aspirations of more working class parents for their children have helped to increase the social and political pressures for improved educational services. The school is fast becoming a powerful socializing force. The full potential of a child is more likely to be realized as stability in the triangle of relationships between child, parent and teacher is secured. The design of an environment which promotes this is therefore of major importance.

The greatest social change in Britain during the post-war years has been in the quality and character of human relationships. Education has become a matter of personal involvement in an enterprise in which the old hierarchical structures have tended to disappear or become blurred. Authority is wielded humanely and with understanding. The fears of superior authority, of not being able to perform adequately, or of venturing into the unconventional, have largely disappeared.

[1] HALF OUR FUTURE (The Newsom Report) HMSO 1963; CHILDREN AND THEIR PRIMARY SCHOOLS (The Plowden Report) HMSO 1967

13

A partnership has evolved in which education officers and inspectors try to solve the problems of the schools with headteachers, in a spirit of mutual trust and regard. Teachers have come down from their pedestals and involve themselves in the experiences and searchings of their children. They support and strengthen each other's weaknesses, and combine their skills. Parents are more welcome in the schools than formerly, and are beginning to play an active role in their affairs. A school building should therefore help to bring people (teachers, children, parents, and helpers) together in normal social interactions, not keep them apart in artificially contrived groups. This 'warms' the educational processes.

Over fifty years ago, distinguished educators were telling us how children learn, but it is only during the last twenty years or so that we have applied widely the principles they established. These are: that education is an active process of learning by exploration and discovery, and that knowledge is only absorbed and interpreted in so far as its relevance is understood. Children also learn as much from each other and from agencies outside the school as they do from teachers in school. Learning is a personal and individual matter. In infant schools, the 'free day' and the 'integrated curriculum' have replaced an organizational structure based on fixed periods of time devoted to specific subjects. Creative synthesis has supplanted the former analytical approach to the curriculum, and cut right across the conventional distinctions between subjects. What children do should make sense to them through its very wholeness.

On the other hand, older juniors of nine and ten years of age are now beginning to need teachers with special knowledge and experience of biology physical science, mathematics, modern languages music and other branches of the arts. Assisted by the rich resources which a good supply of books apparatus and tools, radio, television, films, and tapes can bring to their learning, some children are now able to grasp concepts and achieve skills hitherto considered beyond them. In short, some of them are putting away childish things rather earlier nowadays, much as their elders may regret this.

The implications of these changes for primary school design have only been fully realized within the last few years. A primary school is now seen as a market place of educational opportunities for the children, the variety of which is only matched by the variety of life which will be open to the present generation of schoolchildren. It is no longer a matter of designing for classes of a given size, each occupying a separate room and following a clearly defined programme. Such an approach immediately limits the choices available to the separate classes, except at enormous cost. Architects should be designing for an ever increasing variety of inter-connected activities, readily available to groups of children and their teachers for the exploration of the problems they set themselves.

Changes in attitudes and objectives In the 1930s and 1940s, great emphasis was placed on the physical standards of buildings. Particular attention was paid to the improvement of heating, ventilation and lighting. Little attention was given to educational trends. From 1950 onwards, however, there emerged in England a few groups of architects whose interests went a good deal beyond the application of their formal principles and practice to the design and building of primary schools. They came to realize that ideas about the education of young children were changing, and that teachers were wanting to use their buildings differently from the way they had a few years before. Architecture is a social art, these architects were saying, and it begins with people; with the kind of school life they wish to create; with the new relationships between teachers and children; with the new ways of learning being explored. This approach could not be made by the 'jack-of-all-trades' type of architect who claims to design and build anything. The architects being described studied trends in education, and soaked themselves in the subject; they established special working relationships with far-seeing educators and the most successful practising teachers in order to create a richer life and a more varied learning environment for children. The dialogue was a continuing one, and allowed school design to evolve round changing educational ideas. The involvement with people has produced, in the architects, attitudes towards design and solutions to some current technical problems, which differ from those found in other countries. These are dealt with under the three headings of 'flexibility' 'variety', and 'environment'.

Flexibility

When the emphasis in education was upon instruction and the work done by children was under the close supervision of their teachers, the closed classroom was a suitable unit of school accommodation It still has a purpose where acoustic isolation is essential to the quality of the teaching (as in poetry-reading or in critical listening to music) As more varied and active ways of learning were introduced and classes were arranged in groups for the purpose, so classrooms grew in size to cope with this. But as the work became more individual, and the experiences necessary to the children much more varied and sophisticated, so work extended beyond the confines of these large rooms. Today a child's own theme of study necessitates the employment of several learning techniques and the use of an increasing variety of special facilties (See the case study of the Eynsham School, page 48.) The child may also draw on the knowledge and experience of several teachers or other adults. The ability to create more 'boxes', or to vary their sizes scarcely contributes to solving current organizational problems in primary schools. Movable walls have a habit of remaining fixed. Today's primary school design problem is to provide for many individual pursuits, while still making it possible for teachers to isolate groups when special tuition is needed.

Modern building technology and science tend to persuade architects towards uniformity of the physical environment. Architects can design a school on the basis of a sealed, factory-type floor, and of uniform ceiling height, air-conditioned and artificially illuminated, and offering high standards of physical comfort. Within this shell, standard partitions can be provided which are movable, enabling the users to change the relative areas of adjacent spaces to meet organizational changes of group or class sizes. However, varying the sizes of groups to be taught in enclosed spaces is no longer the major problem of the primary schools in this country. Such a system gives no more than mechanical flexibility, and has not been welcomed in Britain, because it tends to be expensive and to restrict the learning opportunities of the children. A windowless, shadowless, unchanging physical environment divorces the children's learning from those natural forces which have shaped and conditioned human, animal and plant life, as well as from the aesthetic experiences which changing light alone can bring. British architects have concentrated on a 'built-in' form of educational flexibility, which derives from the variety of the environment and the multiplicity of learning opportunities provided.

Variety

What does 'variety' mean in a British primary school? It is the varied character of the learning environment to which children are exposed in school life, and through which the teacher communicates with them: raw materials, tools, and machines, for children to touch, to handle, and to use; the work of artists and craftsmen to inspire; the works of nature and of science to wonder at. In the final count, it is something imparted to the school's physical environment by the imagination and sensitivity of the teachers; but architects are now providing the means for teachers to do this through the built-in flexibility which arises from a study of what children want to do, and the way they work. What are these?

Children must be able to find books when they need them and to squat in a comfortable, quiet place and browse over them. They may need to take them away to a table or bench where they are doing some writing or perhaps constructing a model. Books should be able to penetrate everywhere. Young children like to huddle in small groups to listen to a story or discuss experiences, and for this they like to feel 'contained' and 'cosy' (they communicate better when they can see each other's faces). They listen to tapes or watch films or slides either individually or in groups. They will write at great length and sometimes with considerable feeling and sensitivity, and for this they will seek a working place of their own. They are avid collectors of 'treasure', and this can be purposefully channelled; almost everything is grist to their mill. They are great explorers of almost any environment: streams, meadows, woodlands, the sea shore, waste dumps, junk yards, building sites, parks, streets, shops, garages, and workshops and factories within the range of their understanding. They love to arrange their collections on table tops or display them on walls—to label, systematize and record their discoveries. They are curious about all kinds of tools, contrivances, and materials, and are eager to use them in developing ideas of their own. They work in paper, cardboard, wood, sheet metal, wire, plastics, plaster, soft stone, fabrics and other soft materials, and use waste boxes and containers of all shapes and sizes. Above all they enjoy finding out, experimenting, and confirming for themselves; in this they will use magnets of many kinds, batteries, switches, wire, light bulbs, motors, clocks and watches, thermometers, barometers, inclined planes, pendulums, pulleys, and a great variety of measuring instruments. They use musical instruments and write much of their own music. They express themselves in pictures and patterns carried out in a variety of media. They find cooking, and eating what they have prepared, particularly enjoyable. Plants and living creatures fascinate them. The range of experiences is being continually extended, and now far exceeds what can be accommodated within a confined class space. (See the case studies on Eynsham school, page 48 and on St Thomas of Canterbury School, Manchester, page 61.)

The principle of sharing territory and facilities, though not welcomed at first, is increasingly accepted by teachers as they appreciate the variety it offers. They cooperate willingly, by each making some special contribution to the whole. This might be thought of as the British equivalent of the much more highly organized and programmed forms of team teaching now practised in other countries. In Britain the children are exposed naturally to learning experiences, pursue work of their own choice, and are given help when they need it. To avoid all the frustrations of hopeless clutter, space must have a 'geography' which the children can understand; an arrangement of books, tools, materials and apparatus, which makes for efficient working and helps the children to achieve their purposes; and a variety of working positions—standing at a bench, writing at a table, reading in a comfortable chair, squatting on the floor—suited to the many jobs which children do.

Environment
Emotional reaction to the character of space is as strong as the purely physical reactions to standards of warmth, light, sound, and air movement. The former is a subjective matter, one might contend, and therefore not strictly within the realms of architecture.

But such characteristics often determine the quality of communication between the 'people' in a school, and are therefore of vital importance in education. Some architects in the past have gone no further than producing a uniform, all-purpose clinical space for the education of young children bearing all the marks of impersonal institutionalized life. But education owes a great deal to those groups of architects previously mentioned, who have concerned themselves with the whole environment in which children live and grow. Communication is impaired by the unsympathetic quality of an environment for a particular activity. In primary school, individual children might say:

I want to read quietly in a small space where I can curl up and feel cosy and comfortable.

I am trying to find enough floor space to make a model of London Airport.

I am modelling wild animals I have seen at the zoo and I shall be making a mess.

I like to try out tunes on musical instruments and I don't want someone to tell me to be quiet.

I am looking for a quiet place to write my book about the planets.

I want to invent dances.

I am doing some experiments with wheels, cog wheels and pulleys and I want a place to hang them up.

I want to listen to this tape about mountain climbing.

I want to paint a portrait of Jean.

And so it goes on.

Sensitive architects can impart to working space a character which promotes a particular attitude to a job done in it; privacy for quiet study, intimacy for quiet group-listening; workmanlike and messy spaces; clinical spaces to cope with noise. The colour, texture and furnishing of the walls; the cold, warmth or hardness of floors; carpets, rugs and cushions; tables to read and write at, and working surfaces for many kinds of jobs; chairs, stools and bench seating, hard and upholstered, for adults as well as children; all these contribute to the quality and character of the environment. Light from the windows, casting oblique shadows and giving shape and texture to the many interesting objects and materials within the building; delightful prospects of clouds, trees and building shapes seen from the inside; all these constitute the learning environment which we call school.

But the outstanding feature of some of the new primary schools in this country is the way in which the great variety of working areas interlock, and penetrate each other, so that no child is far away from a facility he requires or a person he needs. The school becomes a country to be discovered and explored. It provides many points where adults can be teachers, student teachers, helpers, parents, welfare workers, artists and craftsmen, all playing their part in the teaching and learning. The whole is a complex relationship of people and spaces. For instance, in the most recent schools, there are few doors, as these stop the flow of ideas from imaginative people who initiate them or from gifted children who develop and extend them.

Changes in administrative attitudes

Facing the post-war problem

Administrators, both national and local, have played a most significant role in primary school building. First, they saw the social benefits which would accrue from spreading school building capital resources more widely. The problem was how to pass the wine round to more people without having to dilute it. Secondly, they realized that this problem could only be resolved by a combined effort on the part of architects, educators and administrators, and they set out to adjust the machinery of government administration[1] to encourage this

[1]See, in this series, THE GOVERNMENT OF EDUCATION by Maurice Kogan

21

liaison. The movement was initiated, in abou 1948, by such local education authorities as th County of Hertfordshire and the City of Coventry Here, architects were observing children at work i primary schools and were consulting teachers abou the kind of learning facilities they wished to creat for them. Teachers were beginning to exploit mor fully the natural ways in which children learn an were demonstrating that the whole environmen both physical and human, educates. New ap proaches to primary school design, centring on th needs of the children themselves, were therefor made. Here, and elsewhere, authorities were als facing the problem of unprecedented growth of th child population, following the Second World War and the rapid development of new urban com munities. The provision of schools for these chilc ren was a race against time, and a severe strai upon resources of all kinds. Such problems coul only be resolved through combining the expertis of all those concerned with the design, constructio: and economics of school building. The local author ities most successful in this task were those whic established combined professional teams draw from their Education and Architects' Department to tackle the problems.

Collaboration

In order to spread some of the ideas initiated by few local authorities, and to assist others in solvin some of the pressing problems of school building in 1949 the Ministry of Education reorganized it own Architects and Buildings Branch, and estab lished its Development Group to work in clos collaboration with local education authorities. It objectives were twofold: to build new schools whic would keep pace with changing educational though and practice, and to secure the maximum possibl educational value for the money expended on schoc building. Collaboration is not just the educato stating his demands, the architect meeting ther in his design, and the administrator finding th means to erect the building. It involves each of these in an active and informed understanding of the others' interests, and requires from each a readiness to compromise for the common good. The administrator must try to remove irksome or inhibiting regulations, and must steer a sensible course between economy in the expenditure of public money and meeting the full needs of education. The architect must have a genuine sympathy for educational objectives and ideals, and must design not merely a school building but the best possible total environment for the living and learning of young children. The educator, while maintaining his ideals, must occasionally temper his demands to ease the architect's technical problems, and must be prepared to examine with him unconventional design solutions which make more productive use of the space available.

Cost

It is only possible to touch upon the economic aspects of school building in this booklet. Nevertheless, it should be noted that the combined attack made in the 1950s on the cost per place of new buildings, resulted in better designed and more successful primary schools. From the architects of the 1930s we inherited primary schools which consisted of long rows of similar, box-like classrooms, separated by storage rooms and arranged along corridors. They were generally single-storey buildings. The long corridors led to cloakrooms and lavatories which were at a considerable distance from the classrooms, and to the hall, dining-room and administrative offices. Such schools sprawled about their sites and lacked essential cohesion. They were difficult to organize, and small children were even known to lose their way in the maze of corridors. It was not unusual to find sixty per cent of the total floor area given to non-teaching space. What uneconomic instruments of education these schools were! The cost attack set out to reverse this trend and to design at least sixty per cent of the total

floor area as usable teaching space. Early develop
ment work sought to make primary schools les
institutional and more domestic in character. A
whole classes move about very little, long traffi
routes for them were hardly necessary. Lowerin
the heights of ceilings brought the buildings int
scale with the children, and made them much mor
homelike. This reduced considerably the cubic con
tent of the buildings. A more compact arrangemen
of the classrooms, each with its own storage, cloak
room and sanitary facilities, greatly reduced th
total floor area. Though early development wor
reduced the cost per place from £200 to £140, it in
creased classroom sizes from 500 to 700 and 80
square feet. Nowadays, the merging of the class
rooms, the sharing of space by teachers and thei
classes, the much more fluid arrangement c
facilities, and the almost total elimination of pur
circulation space, have brought about a furthe
increase in the proportion of space available fo
learning and teaching.

The second attack on cost has been throug
methods of cost analysis and cost planning. Thes
techniques have emerged through comparativ
building studies made by quantity surveyors. Jus
as we must get greatest educational value fc
money out of every square foot of space, so we mus
know where each penny goes on the building. Tech
niques for measuring the cost (to a fraction of
penny per square foot) of the various elements of
building have been devised and these can be con
pared. Thus, the cost per square foot of floor are
of separate building elements, such as the fram
the walls and facings, the windows and doors, th
heating installations and the electrical work, ca
be determined and compared as between one pr
mary school building and another. Comparisons r
veal what is economical and what is extravagan
what can be afforded and what cannot. Thus, th
deployment of cost in a building can now be planne
from the outset.

The industrialization of building

Traditional methods of building were far too slow to keep pace with the rising school population, so that an attack on the technical aspects of building became a matter of urgency. Twenty years ago, prefabrication was largely regarded as a temporary expedient to meet a crisis. Industrialized building is now a social necessity in England, especially in the public sector of the economy where there is increasing pressure to provide decent living conditions and better social amenities for all members of the community. Buildings produced in this way should not be less good than traditional ones and need not produce the monotonous, uniform landscapes of standardized buildings that stultify minds and hearts.

Many local education authorities have now organized themselves into school building consortia to design building systems, standardize components, get these manufactured in bulk, and arrange for their delivery on time according to a predetermined building programme. This approach does not standardize school buildings. The various systems have architects with a great measure of choice of components and finishes, so that thev are still able to produce buildings varied in shape, size and character. Although industrialized building systems are now used widely, they are the means, not the end, of school building. Architects using them are able to bring to primary schools the great variety of facility demanded by the most recent educational practice, and to design round the special needs of a particular school community.

Collaboration with the teaching profession

Most local education authorities have now established arrangements for consulting their teachers about changes in school organization and teaching practice, and about the best use to be made of new furniture and equipment. Sometimes this is done through a formally constituted teachers' advisory committee, to which the authority refers educational questions. This involve agreement by consensus, and is often too slow moving to keep pace with change, unless it is well informed in matters of educational innovation Other authorities use more informal methods of channelling ideas to architects, and of keeping them in touch with new developments. Above all architects themselves must have direct access t the best teaching practice within their areas an should be able to talk informally with teachers Some education authorities have been slow to make changes, and have not been ready to accept new approaches to school design until these have been assessed and confirmed by practising teacher working in the new buildings. Unfortunately ther is a time lag of between three and four years be tween a new concept expressed in an architect' first sketch plan and the smoothly working schoc to be assessed. The gap may be as much as six year by the time the authority has built a similar schoo and educational change will have marched on Provided a new concept has evolved from a con tinuing dialogue between first-class practising teachers and imaginative architects, there shoul be no reason to suspect it and every reason t examine it.

The Oxfordshire County Education Authority[1]

A good example of the collaborative method o working is to be found in Oxfordshire, where collaboration in primary school design has evolve which is almost unique in public administration i this country. A mainly rural county with a dis persed population, three quarters of its two hundre or so primary schools are village schools providin for up to fifty or sixty children. A few larger school are to be found in the small market towns. Whe the Eynsham Primary School opened in 1967 it wa revolutionary in the form of organization i assumed and in the degree of teacher cooperatio it demanded. It came as a shock to many teacher outside Oxfordshire and could not be readil

[1]See also, in this series, A RURAL SCHOOL by Robert T. Smith

accepted by them. How did it come about?

In the middle 1950s, as the emphasis in education moved from teaching to learning, there began a movement to establish local groups of primary teachers to discuss their objectives and to exchange experiences about new methods of working. It started with informal meetings, arranged by the authority's officer and adviser for primary education. These were warmly welcomed by the teachers, working in an area where it is easy to feel isolated from the main stream of events. Other education officers and advisers joined in, and visits were exchanged between one school and another. Ideas spread, as teachers made bold experiments in creating a new kind of learning environment within their old buildings. At the same time, the authority wished to carry out modest improvements to old school buildings, which they were able to discuss with the teachers, and were experimenting with a new range of furniture. The raising of standards of work also came under discussion, and conscious efforts were made to improve the quality of aesthetic experience for the children, by exposing them to good design and fine craftsmanship in many and varied forms. The response of the children was tremendous and their work blossomed. As a result, the county nurtured a breed of teachers who were not only receptive to new ideas, but who initiated and developed them. Many architects were inspired by the vitality of the work in the schools.

For many years, therefore, the county has been in the van of progress in primary school design, innovation emerging from evolving educational and social philosophies. The new village school at Finmere (page 33) set the whole trend of primary school design for the 1960s. Within its small compass it provided a greater measure of learning opportunity for fifty children than ever achieved before. It set the pattern for cooperative teaching, children of all ages sharing in the facilities provided. Though Eynsham (page 48) was the logical outcome for a much larger school (320 pupils), it took considerable

courage to launch it upon the public, rejectin
as it did the traditional notion of a primary scho
as a collection of fixed classes, each with its ow
teacher and class space. It demanded a high level
teacher cooperation and a willingness to acce
'mixtures' of children of all ages and abilitie
However, the concept was based on successful soci
experiments already made in smaller schools, an
the more visionary teachers were quite prepar
for it.

The administrative process for school buildi
in the county is simple and effective. An assista
education officer acts in liaison with the coun
architect's department. He prepares documents an
convenes meetings. The county's education office
and advisers draw up a framework of requiremen
for a new school. On this is based the first sket
plan, which is often preceded by discussions b
tween education officers and architects abo
educational trends. The plan is then studied by t
Director of Education and his officers. Revisio
are suggested and discussed with the architec
and sensible compromises reached. A revised sket
plan is then sent, with a request for comments,
other interested parties; ie, the local school ma
agers and headteacher (if appointed), and an
specialists who normally advise the authority.
final sketch plan is then drafted, which is su
mitted to the Education Committee for its a
proval. Oxfordshire's achievements in prima
school building largely rest on the informed opi
ion of its teachers, which in turn is created
education officers and architects. One spurs t
other in a cycle of consultation and collaboratic

2 Recent Trends in Primary School Design

There is, in many adult minds, a fixed image of a school building—a grey, gritty asphalt playground surrounded by high walls or iron railings; blocks of lavatories and cloakrooms; long corridors with unfriendly doors; rows of classrooms with high windows, and with lines of desks facing the teacher's platform and the blackboard; partitions fretted with small panes of glass; heating pipes, radiators and tall cupboards; green and brown paint and glazed tiles. For over a century, and until the 1950s, elementary school design assumed this inflexible, institutional character, and people appear to have accepted it, like the weather, as inevitable.

But many a forbidding school exterior conceals a warm life within. In many old buildings, imaginative and resourceful teachers, helped by sympathetic education authorities, wage incessant war against adverse physical conditions. Through redecoration and miracles of improvisation, they have transformed their schools into friendly, inviting places. Reference has already been made to the interest such efforts evoked in architects who were making communities of people their starting point in design, and no study of the evolution of primary school design in recent years would be complete without some record of the changes wrought in the physical environment of schools by teachers themselves. They were the direct consequences of two very strong, but inter-related, movements.

Firstly, they were the outcome of the changes in personal relationships which teachers wished to

bring about in the classrooms. Physically, t
classrooms lost their 'front' and 'back' and t
teachers moved everywhere. Desks or worktabl
were so arranged that the children looked into ea
other's faces rather than at the backs of ea
other's necks. Children thus shared experienc
and helped each other, and communication becam
personal and intimate. Teachers were changing t
gaunt, impersonal, institutional classroom into
learning environment which in scale and charact
was domestic and homelike. They introduced dome
tic furnishings and equipment: a rug, a couch, a
upholstered chair, colourful curtains, and t
materials, tools and utensils of home—all th
helped to warm relationships and remove fear
The more discerning teachers created homi
points to which children gravitated when they fe
in need of human support.

Secondly, there were the physical consequenc
of the more active approach to learning now bei
pursued, and the need to increase the range a
variety of educational opportunity for the childre
This is an insatiable and continuing demand whi
is bringing about revolutionary changes in scho
design. It first expressed itself in the urgent ne
for more floor space, which the teachers satisfi
simply by opening the classroom doors and letti
out the children into neighbouring corridor
entrance halls, cloakrooms, stores, dining-room
outside workspaces, and any other areas they cou
conveniently press into service. In some school
corridors became workshops and, in others, qui
writing and book reference spaces. The interesti
discovery was made that people could still circula
through these areas without disturbing unduly t
work of the children. Concentration and a sense
purpose are great insulators, and the children we
generally in these spaces because they were wor
ing at a job of their own choosing. Two desi
innovations resulted from this. In order to redu
the frequency of movement along corridors, was
ing and sanitary facilities were planned in dire

association with classrooms. Broad corridors were deliberately designed as working extensions to the classrooms, and were sometimes equipped with sinks and worktops. Wide, folding classroom doors were installed to help the flow of activity. These eventually evolved into classrooms of between 800 and 1,000 square feet in area, with circulation through the open ends, the folding doors having been removed. The Hertfordshire County Architect pioneered many of these developments.

There followed a second phase of change in which the improvisations of the teachers became much more sophisticated. A flood of books, materials, tools, gadgets, mechanical devices, spare parts, and sundry useful objects, poured into the classrooms and were in constant use by the children. It wasn't a matter of putting them away in a storage space to be retrieved when needed, but of arranging the teaching space to absorb them systematically, so that they could be found and used immediately they were required. Cupboards, pianos, bookshelves, screens, benches and other pieces of furniture were used to define functional spaces for specific types of work—sitting-rooms, kitchens, workshops, libraries, museums, bases for exploration and investigation—where the required tools, apparatus and materials could be found and essential information displayed. This alerted designers to the great need for mobility in school furnishing. Easily movable storage cupboards of many types, bookshelves, display units and space dividers soon appeared on the market. As children lost their individual workplaces, so mobile units, incorporating deep plastic trays for the storage of their personal possessions, were designed.

A few teachers realized that the aesthetic environment to which children are exposed is important to their growth. They therefore turned their attention to the quality of the workspaces they were creating. The backs of cupboards were lined with attractive materials or with pin-up board. Painted lattice and white corrugated cardboard were frequently used to form special work bays, and these were often given a domestic character by the skilful use of printed fabrics and wallpapers: for example, in sitting-rooms and library spaces. Fabrics and friezes, printed or painted by the children themselves, became common, and the work of artists and craftsmen was displayed alongside that of the children. Plants, animals and natural sculptured forms all found a place in this *milieu* of learning, and classrooms became not only workshops but shop windows of the world. Teachers were trying to impart to all these special work areas a character appropriate to their particular functions. In response to this, architects began to study how they could design schools which would be more effective instruments in the skilful hands of these sensitive teachers.

Developments in the curriculum and in the fields of investigation explored by the children also affected design. Developments in the teaching of modern languages demanded efficient arrangements for the use of visual and auditory equipment by groups of children. Bays for the investigation of mathematical problems and for experimentation in the physical sciences were created by enterprising teachers. There would be apparatus for investigating shapes, space and volume; pulleys, wheels and gears for the study of machines; simple equipment for exploring magnetism and electric circuitry. Areas were also given over to living sciences and the discoveries within the natural environment of the school neighbourhood. Add to this an infinity of creative pursuits in which children engage—their painting, carving, modelling, building and inventing; their music making, drama and dancing; their literary efforts in prose and poetry. The whole building then emerges as a complex physical framework, becoming ever more complicated as the potential of children is more fully realized through the inspiration of their teachers.

A few primary school designs have been selected for special study, to illustrate the trends of development in England during the last twelve years. In all of them, architects and educators have worked in close collaboration, and in each of them significant design innovations have emerged to meet new educational demands. Two examples of rehabilitating old school buildings to match present-day requirements are included. One is merely the modest improvement of a village school, but the other represents the full remodelling of an old London primary school to meet modern building and educational standards.

Finmere The opportunity to build a new village school rarely occurs in Britain, because population growth is occurring mainly on the outskirts of large towns. It was such a school, however, built in 1958–59, which set the course of primary school design for at least a decade. The school was built to serve the villages of Finmere, Mixbury and Newton Purcell in Oxfordshire. Prior to this, the three villages had their own tiny schools, accommodated in very old buildings quite unsuitable for their purpose.

ne of a series of work recesses provided for the younger children

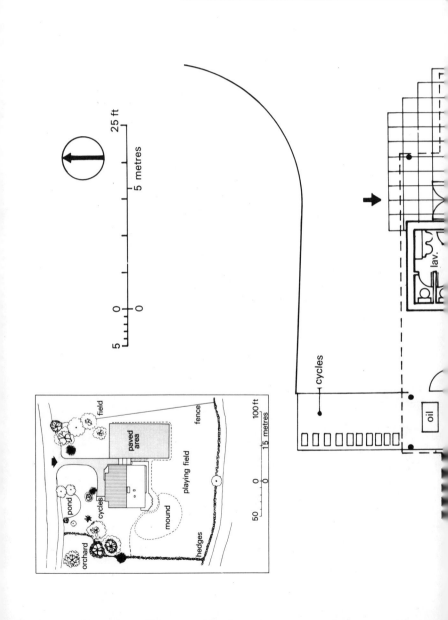

25 ft

5 metres

5   0   5 metres

cycles

lav.

oil

field

paved area

playing field

mound

cycles

pond

orchard

hedges

fence

50   0   100 ft

0   15 metres

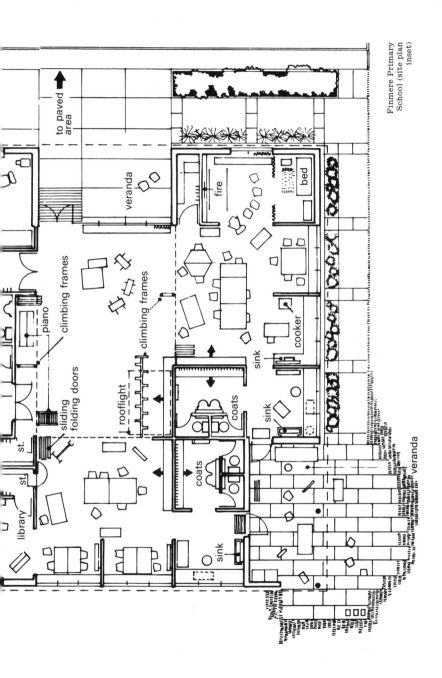

to paved area

veranda

fire

bed

climbing frames

climbing frames

rooflight

piano

sliding folding doors

coats

coats

coats

cooker

sink

sink

sink

sink

st.

st.

library

veranda

Finmere Primary School (site plan inset)

To imaginative architects, the design problem that of compressing into the space of a village school an almost infinite variety of educational and social facilities for the children, was an innovative force in itself. The Oxfordshire Education Authority was eager to experiment. The architects had already seen the great variety of educational experiences being improvised by teachers in the many village schools of this rural county. Instead of offering the conventional, anonymous, box-type classroom solution, they deliberately broke up the space into a number of linked learning areas, each with a special function and character which positively invited a particular activity. Though the design aroused the criticism that architects were determining an educational pattern, all decisions were made in close collaboration with the authority's officers and teachers. Variety of educational opportunity was the keynote of the whole design and the object was to produce a building which, in the hands of discerning teachers, contributed to the processes of learning and maturing.

A village school is a small, closely knit community in which each child is known by the rest. In this school, there are about fifty children, ranging in age from five to eleven years, and their two teachers. They work in small groups or as individuals, each making his own contribution to the life of the school; the old help the young, the strong help the weak, and the clever ones help those who are slow. The children group and re-group according to their ability, age and interests, and design must take account of a frequently changing work pattern. Children may carve in wood or stone, model in clay, construct in varied materials, collect, spin, dye and weave their own wool, draw and paint, bake and cook, explore streams and hedgerows, browse among books, write prose and poetry, calculate, estimate and investigate, and any or all of these activities may be followed at one and the same time. Village children are quite used to getting on with the job they have set out to do and a visitor to this type of school is unaware of the teacher 'teaching'. She gives unobtrusive help and advice when it is needed. Parents join in school life, and village as well as school parties and celebrations take place in the school.

The two diagrams detail the facilities provided. The site of about one-and-a-half acres is laid out for the enjoyment of children, the pond and such trees as existed having been retained. There is open access to it from the village and children are able to enjoy it to the full both in and out of school hours. The work of the school often involves the amenities of the site and even the village itself. The building has been planned as a series of linked working areas, each with a degree of privacy but related to the whole. Each has a character of its own, imparted by the wall and floor finishes, the lighting, and by the furniture and equipment.

The sitting-room

There is a sitting-room, furnished in plain fashi... with rocking chair, low table, a window seat, cu... tains and rugs, and a bedroom alcove for a child rest when need be. Another such space provides kitchen, with cooking stove, sink, suitable worki... surfaces, and storage for equipment. Such spac... are not mere toys provided for children's pla... There is a realism about them which allows t... children to work as they would with their paren... on the scale and in the manner of their own hom... There is also a well-stocked library with amp... shelving and wide walls, a mobile book troll... tables and chairs, curtains and rug. Two sm... workshop spaces open on to an outside cover... veranda where the children can build on a larg... scale. Each has a large sink, a fixed worktop wi... a washable plastic finish, and a bench. In additi... there are a number of small group project or stu... areas. As can be seen from the larger plan, t... 'private' spaces open on to larger work areas a... are finally linked to an open space sufficiently lar... for a group of children to engage in drama or dan... or climb ropes and ladders. This has direct acc... to the asphalt playground outside, where mo... physical work may develop.

The building offers considerable flexibility... use. It may be divided into three teaching spac... each of about 600 square feet, by drawing across t... folding partitions provided. As there are norma... only two teachers, such an arrangement is scarce... necessary. By closing one of the partitions only,... is possible to divide the building into one lar... working space of 1,200 square feet, and another 600 square feet. Finally, with the opening of bo... partitions, the building offers a large working ar... and access for all children to the total opportu... ties provided. The cooperative teaching meth... which have since developed require that bo... partitions remain open for the major part of t... teaching programme. For the full social devel... ment of the children, this is now found to be t... happiest arrangement.

Small numbers, a wide age-range, and considerable diversity of interests and abilities among the children, have joined to give this, and some other village schools, a special character in which almost everything is shared, and close relationships develop throughout the community of teachers and children. Skills are pooled, experiences are shared, and all play their part in the education of each other.

Brize Norton Concurrently with the design of Finmere, the Oxfordshire Education Authority and its teachers, assisted by the County Architect, were looking at some of their old schools to see what modest improvements to the buildings and ingenuity on the part of the teachers could achieve in giving them a more informal and homelike character. One such example is the Brize Norton village school, a lofty stone building with heavy mullioned windows, erected in 1871. Alterations to the fabric of such buildings present difficult and costly physical problems. Nevertheless, a large window was lowered to ground level to give access to an outside working area, and a partition wall was removed. Part of the ceiling was lowered to reduce the scale of the interior. The installation of a cooking stove and a sink, the building of some low wall seating and wall storage, and the provision of new tables, chairs and mobile storage units by the local authority, all assisted in the transformation. The headmaster created a sitting-room by building a light partition and bringing in a sofa, a rug and a low table. An excellent library space was formed similarly. The outcome was a fluid arrangement of learning areas offering a variety of educational experience for the forty to fifty children in attendance. At the same time, improvements were made to the kitchen, cloakroom and sanitary facilities. Though the total space is a little cramped compared with Finmere, it represented a considerable step forward in the adaptation of old buildings to new educational demands at modest cost to the authority. This is

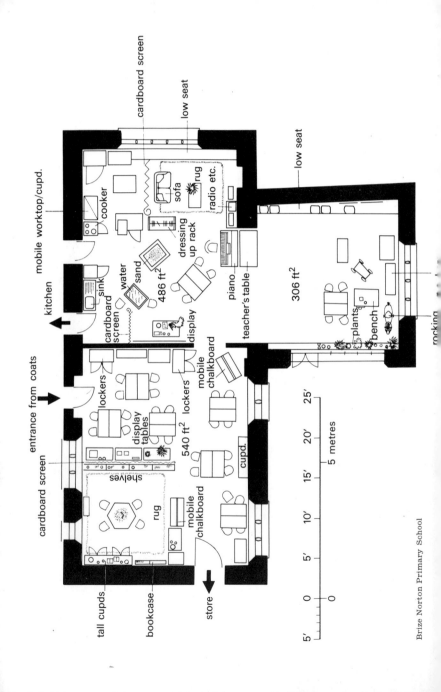

cardboard screen

low seat

low seat

mobile worktop/cupd.

cooker

sofa

rug

radio etc.

dressing up rack

kitchen

sink

water

sand

486 ft²

piano

teacher's table

306 ft²

cardboard screen

display

plants

bench

rocking

entrance from coats

lockers

mobile chalkboard

display tables

lockers

540 ft²

cupd.

cardboard screen

shelves

rug

mobile chalkboard

tall cupds

bookcase

store

5'   0   5'   10'   15'   20'   25'

0   5 metres

Brize Norton Primary School

but one instance of many improvement schemes to be found within the same county area.

Eveline Lowe, London Changes in education techniques stemming from a deeper understanding of the ways in which children learn and grow, were not confined to small village schools. In some large urban schools, experiments had already been made in introducing family patterns of organization within the normal class structure, and in increasing the variety of learning experiences for the children. Many of the primary schools in the cities of Bristol and Nottingham had organized themselves in this way for some years, and were in a position to assess its value. Its implications for primary school building had not been studied, however, and by the early 1960s such an investigation became a matter of urgency. In 1963, the Central Advisory Council for Education (England), under the Chairmanship of Lady Plowden, was beginning its enquiry into the whole area of primary education. It was therefore timely that a research and development group from the Architects and Buildings Branch of the Department of Education and Science should look into the objectives and practice of those teachers who were advancing the frontiers of primary education, and should then design and build an urban primary school to further their aspirations. It was opened in 1966.

The Eveline Lowe Primary School was built on an unpromising, irregular site in south-east London and was designed in collaboration with Inner London Education Authority officers, architects and teachers. It is in an old built-up area of the city, close to commercial undertakings and busy traffic highways, where there are few adult amenities and none for children. Here parents need the support of good nursery, as well as primary school, facilities. The school was planned to provide 320 places, covering an age range of three-and-a-half to nine years. This unusual range lent opportunities for experiment with multi-age groupings

covering the nursery/infant age span and th
infant/junior age span. Children of ten and eleve
years were to be accommodated in adapted ol
premises close by. The architects were asked t
include in their investigations the furniture
furnishings and equipment required to meet new
trends, and so to design the school that parents
helpers, students, and part-time as well as full-tim
teachers could be involved in its life.

The resulting plan is shown in the diagram. Th
building follows the L-shaped site, and its irregu
larities partially enclose amenity spaces and pla
areas designed for the enjoyment of the childrer
The accommodation is arranged in four areas:

1. Nursery space (spaces A and C);
2. Spaces for children between the ages of five an
eight years (spaces B, D, E and F);
3. The 'output end' of the building for the nin
year-olds and a few children of eight years (spac
G and H);
4. The hall/dining-area complex and administr
tion space.

The accommodation need not be organized in strict accordance with this pattern. It is quite capable of serving other groupings. For example, the nursery as a physically isolated community scarcely accords with some more recent concepts of the primary school society. However, the unit could be equally well used by four-, five- and six-year-olds.

Spaces A and C

Each of the nursery spaces is designed for thirty children. Space A is used by children attending half time only. Space C is predominantly for under-fives, but the group includes a few infants also. Each room has a large, open activity space, off which there is a quiet, carpeted and curtained sitting-room. Space A has a bay for the teacher and helper, where they can receive parents or where an adult can withdraw with two or three children. A pleasant recess for parents is provided in the space linking the two rooms, and a small kitchen provides light meals. A deep veranda with a translucent roof extends the indoor play area outside.

Spaces B, D, E and F

Spaces B, E and F are designed so that the life and work of the children can flow uninterruptedly from one area to another. Although the block can function in three separate classes, each with its own teacher, it is designed equally well for a community of 120 children whose work is shared by three teachers. There are so many 'private' bays and recesses for small working groups that several students, helpers or parents could also share in the work and be absorbed easily into the organization. There are three 'bands' of accommodation. Firstly, a band of quiet working areas offers privacy to class groups. They are carpeted and curtained and have bookshelves and display areas, and their character invites quiet reading and writing. In spaces E and F, the areas are raised and are separated by a small closed room used for remedial group work. Space B

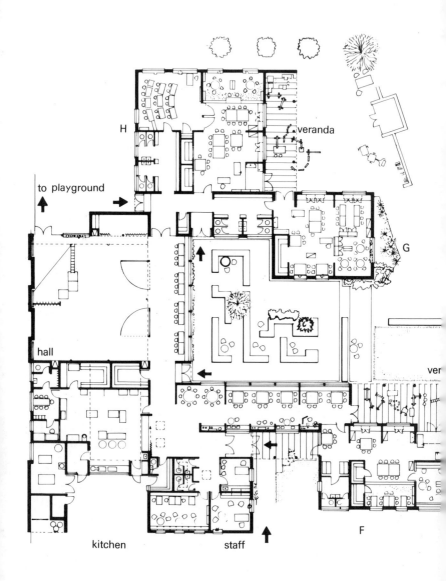

H

to playground

veranda

hall

G

ver

kitchen

staff

F

Eveline Lowe Primary
School (site plan
inset)

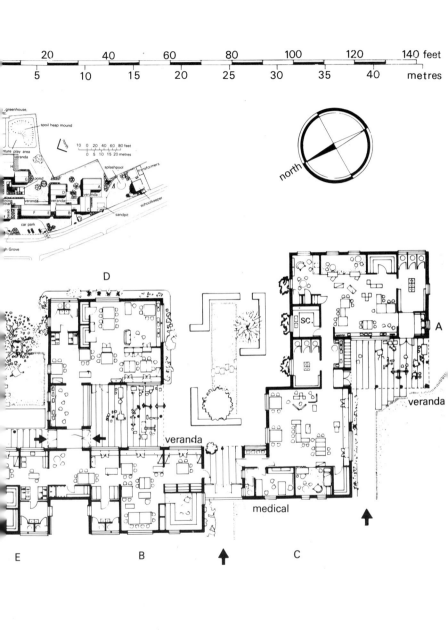

20   40   60   80   100   120   140 feet

5   10   15   20   25   30   35   40   metres

greenhouse
etc.

spoil heap mound

10 0 20 40 60 80 feet
0 5 10 15 20 metres

ature play area
veranda

H

G pond

splashpool

transformers

veranda

ining
tail

veranda   veranda

F   E   B

schoolkeeper

sandpit

car park

gh Grove

D

sc.

A

veranda

veranda

E   B   medical   C

has a quiet 'nest' in which fixed seating for forty children is arranged in two tiers on three sides of the space. The carpet continues up the tiered seating. On one side of it are four bunks for children who need to rest. Secondly, there is a centre band of general working area where children may work at large table surfaces. Finally, there is a line of working bays resembling a row of shops. Three of them have sinks, and easily cleaned worktops, and can be used as workshops for constructing and modelling. Another is a cooking kitchen used by the children. The remainder are equipped with worktop and display surfaces and can be used for investigations in mathematics or science, or as bases for explorations or natural history. One frequently serves as a place where musical instruments can be found and used. Space D has a measure of independence, though it is linked with the other spaces in the main block. It is provided with mobile furniture units, space dividers and other furnishings, the layout of the room being determined entirely by the teacher. All four spaces share generous outdoor working areas which have translucent roofing. This section of the school has been used for experiment with multi-age, family type classes covering all or some of the age range five to eight years.[1]

Spaces G and H

G is a large, squarish space without any subdivisions, and has a range of furnishings which permit alternative room arrangements similar to space D. Space H is designed to accommodate all the sixty pupils of nine years of age who pass out of this section of the school annually. It brings together into a single working community the whole age group and their teachers, some of whom may be part-time. The main space comprises a carpeted library area for quiet study, and a spacious general work area, off which there are recesses given over to science, mathematics and other investigations A section is partitioned from the rest by two wide

[1]See, in this series, SPACE, TIME AND GROUPING by Richard Palmer

doors. The space of about 400 square feet thus formed can be used for teaching a substantial group by the normal methods of exposition, using visual, auditory and other aids, for which it is equipped with full blackout facilities. A group of twenty-five to thirty children needing to practise a skill in quiet conditions or to hold a discussion may meet here. The space was planned particularly for the early teaching of modern languages.

The flexibility achieved by the arrangement of furniture in space G

Hall/dining/administration space

The hall has been planned as a space for physical education, movement, music and drama. For these purposes it is equipped with ladders, ropes, climbing frames, agility apparatus and folding platform units. Children also dine in the south-facing window aisle. But the main dining space is a delightful 'Pullman car' type of arrangement, which also incorporates exhibition space. Here, on a main circulation route, the children are exposed to the work of artists and craftsmen, or to collections of special interest. When not used for dining, the space becomes one of the busiest working areas in the school. Indeed, the school is so designed that almost all the floor area can become productive working space for the children. The school can then be seen as a large workshop of educational opportunities into which is set a number of retreats for quiet, reflective study.

Eynsham The impetus given to primary school design in Oxfordshire by Finmere and other new and adapted schools, and further experiments by venturesome teachers into cooperative teaching arrangements, finally prompted the local authority to make a bold experiment in the planning of a large primary school. This was to be in the growing village of Eynsham, near Oxford, and the school was to accommodate 320 children of five to nine years of age.

Oxfordshire teachers had been experimenting with vertical grouping of children, extending over three, four and five years of the primary school age-span. They were impressed by both its social and educational advantages, but the inflexible, highly compartmented buildings in which they were improvising working arrangements hindered full development. For example, nine-year-olds need access to more elaborate facilities and equipment, as well as a greater range of expertise than do five-year-olds. Sometimes, age or ability groups need to come together for work at their particular level of appreciation. How can design and organization provide for such possibilities and still retain the advantages which accrue from multi-age groupings living and working together? The educators and architects of the Oxfordshire County Council turned their attention to this complex problem, and designed and built the Eynsham school in 1966.

It is greatly to the credit of the local authority's advisers and teachers that they did not compromise in this experiment. As an educational and social concept, its demands on the people who use it are more complex than those of the Eveline Lowe School, assuming as it does that a group of teachers are ready to combine their experience and skill, and to surrender their territorial independence, in the education of a large community of children. They did not ask the architects to retain some physical semblance of classrooms so that, in the event of the experiment not being successful, the school might then revert to a more conventional form of class teaching. The teachers were ready to make this advance and played a major role in the initiation of the scheme. The resulting plan is seen in the diagram on pages 50–1.

Teacher meeting her children in the home base

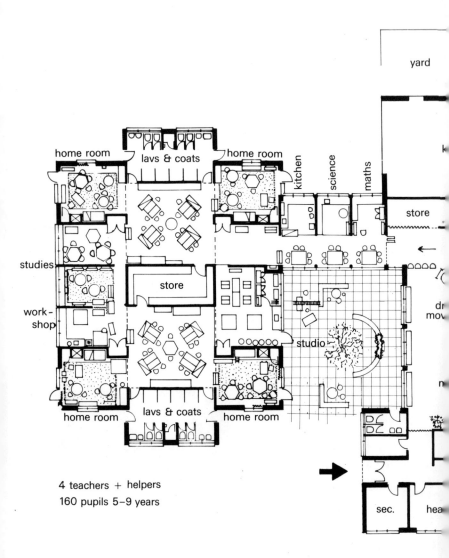

yard

home room

lavs & coats

home room

kitchen

science

maths

store

studies

store

work-shop

studio

home room

lavs & coats

home room

sec.

hea

4 teachers + helpers
160 pupils 5–9 years

Eynsham Primary School

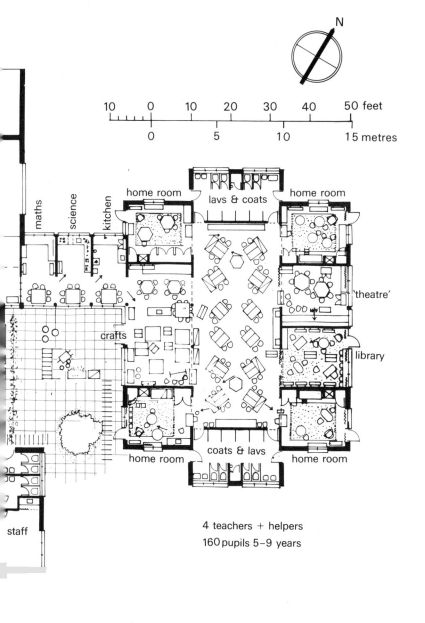

N

10   0   10   20   30   40   50 feet

0   5   10   15 metres

maths

science

kitchen

home room

lavs & coats

home room

'theatre'

crafts

library

home room

coats & lavs

home room

staff

4 teachers + helpers
160 pupils 5–9 years

The hall, dining space, kitchen and administra
tive accommodation comprise a central spine o
building. On each side, and linked with it, is
rectangular teaching block for 160 children. Th
one on the right-hand side of the plan is the mor
interesting, consisting of a large, central area
lighted by clerestory windows and flanked by
number of small spaces which have special fun
tions, and open directly on to the main space. Ther
are no doors to separate or insulate these space
from the central area, though the lower ceilin
height helps to quieten them and give them a fee
ing of privacy. Four of them, one at each corne
serve as sitting-rooms and homing points for eac
of the family groups (five to nine years) into whic
the community is at present basically organize
These are quiet spaces, informally furnished ar
intimate in character. On the right is a carpete
library space with both fixed shelving and movab
book trolleys. Though some seating is provide
many children squat on the carpet to read. Adjoi
ing it is a space, labelled 'theatre' on the pla
which is designed for the direct teaching of twen
or thirty children. It can be blacked out for th
projection of slides and films when so needed. C
the left is a very generous workshop with necessa
services, and appropriate wall and floor finishes a
working surfaces, for a variety of crafts. In the lin
between the hall and this teaching area are thr
workbays, one of which is a cooking kitchen for th
children. The other two have been used recently f
mathematics and archaeological projects.

The teaching space on the left of the centr
spine differs from that on the right in having
central store to divide the main teaching area.
the recent rebuilding of the school, followir
destruction by fire, this store has been omitte
The teachers much preferred the more op
arrangement. Each teaching block is general
staffed by four or five teachers and a helper. Thou
the basic organization is in four family groups, t
children often regroup for special purposes. F

example, at certain times of the day they are divided into five or six age and ability groups for literature, so that all can pursue work at their own levels of development. There are also special groupings for dramatic movement and some aspects of music, such work taking place in the hall. The teachers share in the use of all the accommodation. The main space is frequently subdivided by screens into areas given over to mathematics, language or environmental studies. Even the sitting-rooms sometimes have special functions; for example, the sewing room, the dressing-up room, the games and puzzles room. Though a special area was allocated in the plan to dining, informal dining groups spread themselves everywhere, the meals being trolleyed to these points from the kitchen.

Central work-area looking towards the mathematics section

But for careful preparation and planning, an
very close cooperation among the teachers, chac
could prevail. The whole communications networ
between the teachers and the children is a com
plicated and subtle one. There are messages, in
centives and opportunities everywhere, and th
building plays its part in generating these.

How the unit of accommodation for 160 children is used

1. *Organization by the teaching staff*
The children are divided into four groups, eac
covering the whole age range of five to nine year
Each group has its own teacher, who is responsib
for the personal care and guidance of the childre
overlooks all their work, and takes steps to ensu
that each one develops as fully as possible. Neve
theless, a child will meet and be taught by oth
teachers in the unit as occasion demands. The fo
teachers meet frequently under the chairmansh
of one of them, who acts as convener and leade

They determine such matters as:

the theme of study to be developed over th
next few weeks, and the contribution each w
make (these studies form the major part of th
work and serve to integrate the many skills
be acquired by the children);

the collection and arrangement of sour
material to initiate and inspire the work;

any special layout of the work areas requir
for the study (see the plan on page 50);

the programme of teaching for developing th
theme;

the co-ordination required to give the childr
practice in essential communication skills (e
for young children learning to read);

the regrouping of the children for special work in literature and mathematics at their levels of development, and the programming of such work;

the arrangements for physical education, drama, music and movement, which take place in the hall.

The whole teaching staff of the school meets weekly, under the chairmanship of the headmaster, to clarify objectives, exchange experiences, and discuss modifications in direction or methods that may appear desirable.

2. *Using the accommodation*

The school was visited on a day in January, 1971, and the unit with its accommodation arranged as in the plan on page 50, was working on the theme *Living in winter*. Children soon acquire experience in these studies, and many are able to plan their work with only a little guidance from their teachers. Others need much more support.

On arrival at school, the children take up some aspect of their study immediately, and the unit is a busy place long before the morning session begins. When the day commences officially, the teachers call the groups into their home bases, to deal with registration and other administrative matters. The programme for the day is then discussed and the teacher tells the children of any special teaching taking place in the hall, in the 'theatre' space, or in the home base. Some children may be questioned about the progress of their studies and may be asked to remain in the home base for the teacher to take a closer look at what they have been doing. The rest disperse to the various work areas or to any special teaching groups arranged. The helpers will give a hand with the youngest children, to ensure that they have what they need and to give them an encouraging word. The layout provides a special place where they can go and read and where there will generally be an adult to listen to them.

The children do not invade particular work areas; if a space appears over-subscribed, then they adjust their programmes or seek the help of a teacher in resolving the problem. The programming of the small specialized spaces for science, mathematics and cooking is inevitable.

Most of the children are familiar with the broad plan of study, and understand that their work must embrace many skills and accomplishments. For example, they know that:

(a) their study commences with the investigation of existing source material, and references to books, papers and illustrations, all of which are available to them in the work areas. This collection will grow and extend the range of study as the work proceeds. The various groups work on different aspects of the theme: how animals keep alive in winter (hibernation and migration); how human beings prepare for the winter; winter in other lands; living in winter in former times;

(b) as well as the literary and human interests of the subject, there are mathematical and scientific aspects to be covered: what is meant by freezing; temperature scales; how the body keeps warm; the cost of keeping warm;

(c) craft skills are also involved in the book they make for recording their work, and in their paintings and three-dimensional creations;

(d) within the over-all plan, there are essential skills to be practised and mastered (skills to make them literate and numerate). Assignments for these are to be found in the work areas.

It is customary for the children to meet the teacher for a 'recapitulation' period at the end of the day. They then assess the work they have covered, and discuss anything of special interest which has emerged during the day. This may lead to new thoughts for extending the study.

The periods at the beginning and the end of each day are also 'family' sessions, when the children become aware of their dependence on, and responsibility for, each other. The success of the work depends in no small measure on the willingness of the children to help and support each other. School then becomes a cooperative enterprise on the part of both teachers and children.

Frederick Harrison, Stapleford

This school, designed in the office of the Nottinghamshire County Architect, is for 240 infants, aged five to seven years. It is located on an open site which has little natural protection from the elements. The simple building, almost square in form, encloses a sheltered central court, laid out imaginatively for the work and enjoyment of the children. The impression it gives is of a totality of learning experiences, some inside and some outside, the one flowing into the other on the principle that the whole environment educates.

The school is a good example of the standard of industrialized building in Britain. With its lightweight steel frame, its cladding of handmade clay tiles, and its tall windows, it conveys an impression of fine lines in a domestic form of architecture well suited to be a home for young children. The inside is enchanting. The children move about it freely, for it is essentially a place to discover. The building has been described as 'aggressively domestic', a walk through the school giving the impression of wandering through many private worlds. The insularity of classrooms has been broken down, although (unlike at Eynsham) each teacher tends to operate within a particular class territory. From these bases the teachers have good vision of the many activities taking place within their territory and can keep a kindly, unobtrusive eye on the children's roamings.

The plan opposite provides the key to the organization of the building. There are six classes of about forty children of mixed ages, each with a homing area comprising a quiet sitting-room and a general teaching space. Other specially equipped workbays are shared by the classes, as is the library, and so are the two dining spaces which become busy work areas when not used for meals. The skilful use of pin-up boards and strategically placed spotlights provides the school with delightful display areas. Mobile trolleys, storage cupboards, and screens enable the teachers to set up working bays for particular fields of enquiry as the content and direction of the work change. A whole class may be brought together in the sitting-room for discussion, story or poetry reading. In these spaces, sound-deadening materials have been used such as fabric-covered baffle boards, fitted carpeting and curtains. These rooms are very quiet, without being physically isolated from the general noise of the busy work areas. No teaching area is completely shut off from its neighbour, with the exception of the hall.

Working space for a class group with a quiet homing area on the right

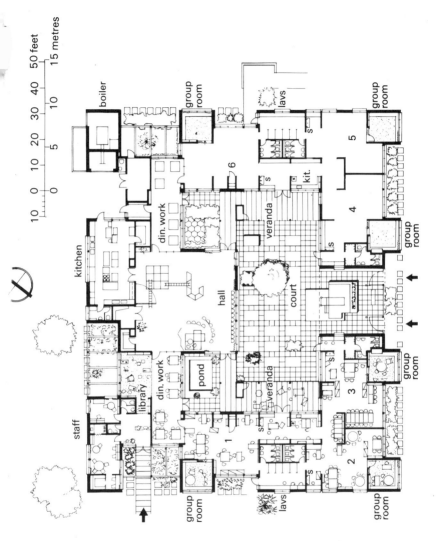

50 feet

15 metres

boiler

group room

lavs

s

group room

5

group room

din. work

6

veranda

s

kit.

kitchen

s

4

hall

court

group room

library

din. work

pond

veranda

3

s

s

staff

s

veranda

1

s

s

group room

2

group room

lavs

The Frederick
Harrison Infants'
School, Stapleford

The revolution in primary school furnishing is nowhere more evident than in this school. This particular building consortium, in conjunction with furniture designers at the Department of Education and Science, has produced its own range of school furniture, with tables of varying shape, size and finish, and seating in great variety—window seats, benches, chairs and low stools, plain or upholstered—as well as generous carpeted space on which the children squat. There are many types of easily moved storage units, some with plastic trays for the children's personal possessions. All the walls have dado rails to protect them from damage by mobile storage units, chairs and tables. Wall colours are neutral over all, but bursts of brilliant colour—crimsons, violets and jades—are provided in the upholstery, in some of the curtains and in the clothing of children themselves. Any building is dead without its users but this one blooms abundantly as the children flock through it.

Fluidity of working space and richness of the learning environment

St Thomas of Canterbury, Manchester

This experimental scheme was promoted by the Schools Commission of the Roman Catholic Diocese of Salford. The school, opened in 1970, is situated in an old part of Manchester, within what is termed an 'educational priority area'; that is, a district where the circumstances of many families are such that the children do not enjoy the social facilities normally necessary to their growth. The building of a new primary school to serve such an area, following immediately on the publication of the Plowden Report, presented the opportunity for a special study of the problems involved. The Schools Commission therefore invited a panel of educators, architects and administrators with first-hand knowledge of the district, to complete a brief for the design of the school, based on the most up-to-date primary school practice and on the findings of the Plowden Report. The building, furnishing and equipment of the school were therefore the subject of a searching study, and the resulting plan is shown on pages 62–3.

Nursery group

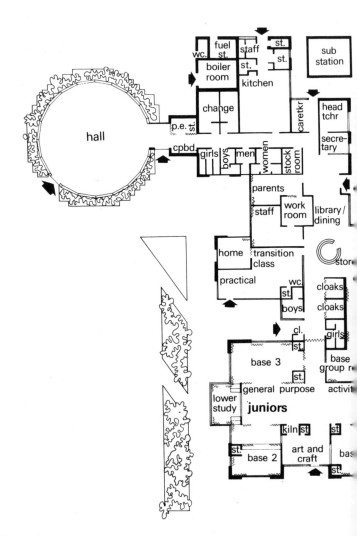

St Thomas of
Canterbury RC
School

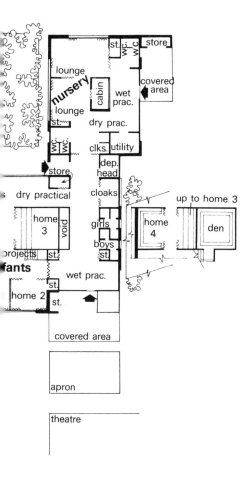

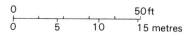
nursery

lounge

cabin

wet prac.

st. wc. wc. store

covered area

lounge

st.

dry prac.

wc. wc.

clks. utility

store

dep. head

dry practical

cloaks

home 3

void

girls

home 4

up to home 3

den

boys

projects st.

st.

fants

wet prac.

st.

home 2 st.

covered area

apron

theatre

At present, the school caters for children up to the age of eleven only. The Panel suggested that the design of the building should look ahead to the time when the long term recommendation of a twelve-plus age of transfer to secondary schools could be implemented, and this has been taken into account. The school provides forty nursery places and 280 places for children of five upwards. Provision for the latter comprises spaces for far more working groups than the usual seven classes of forty children. The accommodation provides bases for nine groups of thirty or so children, or even ten groups of twenty-eight, should the organization demand. The Panel saw the pastoral and tutorial work of the teacher as of major importance, and requested that suitable home bases should be provided for all teachers and groups in their care

Work area for junior pupils. A carpeted area for quiet study is at a raised level

At the same time, they pointed out the social and educational gains to be derived from more frequent contacts between teachers themselves (and from the co-ordination of their several skills) and between children of different ages and abilities. They advised that the building should not restrict movement or the sharing of opportunities and should help to bring people together rather than keep them apart.

The plan defines three zones for the three stages of primary education: a nursery for children up to the age of five, infant space for children between five and eight years, and junior or middle school space for older children up to twelve years of age. The design secures a natural flow of activity between the nursery and infant sections, and permits of experiment in groupings which straddle the age of transfer from one to the other. The nursery area includes two generous sitting-room spaces and a small 'cabin' for intimate story-telling groups. There is ample practical space, in which the children can move freely and engage in a great variety of work. This opens on to a covered outdoor area. In the infant section, comfortable home bases have been provided for four social groups, with access to plenty of well-serviced practical space shared by the teachers and children. Particularly interesting features are the two home bases which can be thrown together to form a small theatre-type space. Below its stepped area, and partly underground, is a 'den' to which fairly large groups may retire. Such accommodation is a spur to the imagination of the teachers and the children.

In designing the accommodation for the junior or middle school, the Panel asked the architects to take special account of the recommendation in the Plowden Report which says: 'If the middle school is to be a new and progressive force it must develop further the curriculum, methods and attitudes which exist at present in junior schools. It must move forward into what is now regarded as secondary school work, but it must not move so far away that it loses the best of primary school education as we know it now.' Children of this age have generally been taught in classes, each by their own teacher and, except for physical education and music, in their own classroom. Today, however, new subjects and new methods are being introduced which call for teachers with special knowledge, who sometimes need special facilities and equipment for their work. The traditional all-purpose classroom therefore no longer suffices. The Panel rejected an organization based on specialist rooms, but suggested the provision of a general workshop area, shared between classes and subjects, 'offering facilities for group work in such fields as science, mathematics, environmental studies and light crafts'. The plan shows such an area, serviced for science and mathematical investigations, and creative work in art and crafts, with storage for apparatus, tools and materials, and plenty of easily cleaned working surfaces. In addition to home bases for four groups, there is a sunken study area which includes individual working carols where tape recorders can be used for practice in modern languages. Separate provision is also made for a transition class of children in need of special care and tuition.

Some aspects of the work, particularly the audio-visual approach to modern language teaching, music, and any teaching in which amplified sound is used, demand a noise-insulated space. This is provided in an acoustically treated, closed space in the centre of the building. Carpeted tiers round a central well provide seating for a large class of children, when need be. The room is equipped with tape recorders, loud speakers and a variety of projectors. The space is in great demand, and is used also for informal drama. Electrical output points for the use of technical apparatus are generously provided through the school.

The promoters were anxious that the school should become an integral part of the community beyond its walls, and that parents should feel we come and at home immediately on entering the building. The entrance is spacious and inviting, and provides an informal waiting area where the school secretary receives parents and visitors. From here, there is a long view of the library/ project area where children are busily at work. But the special feature is a parents' sitting-room which is linked with the staff common room through a shared kitchen and workshop space. Forty to fifty parents already give regular voluntary service to the school, and a harmonious working relationship between teachers and parents is already developing in this difficult area of Manchester. Meals are trolleyed from the kitchen to the L-shaped dining area where the children eat at square tables for eight. When not in use for dining, it affords work space for a variety of projects. Beyond the kitchen is the hall, largely used for physical education, movement and dance, and their associated changing facilities.

There is no timidity about the design of this school. The building not only supports current change in social attitudes and teaching methods but positively invites it. This is already evident in the imaginative response of the teachers to the opportunities it affords them, and the enthusiasm it has aroused in the parents.

Compton, London
While the pace of school building in England allows an increasing proportion of children to attend comparatively new schools, one of the problems of society today is to bring up to date the large stock of old school buildings which are quite unsuited to the new educational demands being made upon them. The problem is most acute in the socially depressed areas of our large towns and cities, where children are often deprived of the normal amenities for growth, so essential to a full and happy childhood. Such a school is the Compton Primary School, a typical three-storey London School Board building, erected in 1881 for the elementary education of children of the poorer classes. It is set among

decayed nineteenth-century terraced housing and old tenements, commercial and industrial undertakings and streets busy with traffic. There are signs of urban renewal in some new blocks of local authority flats being built close by, but the area lacks any open play areas for children.

Thorough remodelling of an old school building to meet current physical and educational standards can cost as much as a new school, and the decision whether to rebuild or remodel is often a difficult one. The remodelling of the Compton school was made the subject of an architectural competition, in which the promoters called for a practical and inventive design for transforming old primary schools within a limited budget (£20,000). This meant discarding expensive physical changes to the building and directing the limited resources towards achieving the greatest educational gain. Some interesting schemes were submitted, full of ideas on how the floor space in this old building could be more fully exploited for the benefit of the children. The object was to redesign the building to provide for 280 children of between five and eleven years of age, as well as thirty nursery places to be operated on a half-time basis.

The original building stood solid and inflexible in the middle of a sea of asphalt playground, surrounded by a high prison-like wall. A block of lavatories was situated across the playground. The ground floor design of the winning entry is shown in the plan on page 70. The right-hand playground, facing southwest, has been designed as an outdoor play space for young children and is linked with the indoor space by deep verandas. To simulate the design features of some of London's newest primary schools, the architect has linked the working areas inside the building by breaking through the walls of the wide corridor and the classrooms, to assist the flow of activity and ideas and sharing of facilities. The right-hand side provides a spacious, self-contained nursery unit with its own entrance, lavatories, parents waiting space, and outside working area. The independent nature of the nursery suite can only perpetuate the separation of the nursery and infant worlds, which scarcely seems desirable any longer. On the left-hand side there are two infant class spaces. The former wide corridor now forms part of their working territory and the whole is designed to foster cooperative working arrangements between the teachers and children concerned. The total space incorporates quiet areas, a variety of workbays and a generous workshop. The two classes share a delightful story-telling den. A new lavatory and cloakroom block for these classes has been added at the south end of the building, close to the children's entrance. A new main entrance from Compton Street leads to the administrative accommodation where the school secretary and headteacher are to be found.

The problems of scale; lofty ceiling and windows, and tiny people and furniture

N

N nursery class
I infant classes
st store
cl cleaning and
   maintenance
   staff

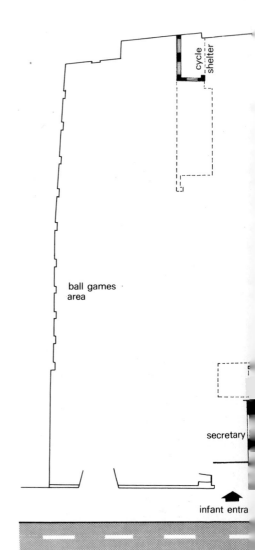

Compton Primary
School ground floor
after remodelling

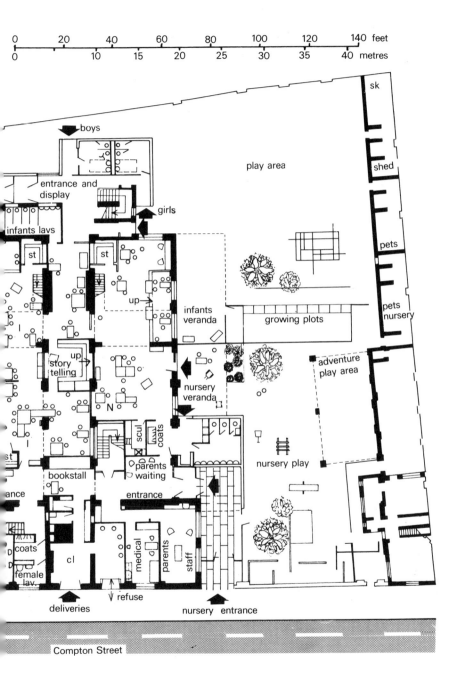

boys

entrance and display

infants lavs

st

st

girls

up

infants veranda

play area

sk

shed

pets

pets nursery

growing plots

story telling

up

N

scul

coats

nursery veranda

adventure play area

bookstall

parents waiting

nursery play

ance

entrance

coats

D

D

female lav.

cl

medical

parents

staff

nursery entrance

deliveries

refuse

Compton Street

New furniture and equipment, offering the same variety, mobility and domestic quality as that found in a new school, complete the picture. But while £20,000 can vastly improve a school, and extend its useful life for say fifteen, or even twenty years, the temptation to spend a great deal more on the environmental conditions is very strong. The lowering of ceilings to reduce the scale of these monumental buildings, the lowering of large windows, the renewal of floors, greater variety of wall finish, the improvement or renewal of main services and kitchen extensions, can build up into a large capital sum. This, in fact, is what has finally happened, and the remodelling of this old building has cost as much as a new school of the same size.

A lively environment created by architect and teachers

It should be pointed out, however, that a new school fulfilling current School Building Regulations could not have been built on this restricted site, and its extension, or the acquisition of an alternative one in the same district, presented the sort of planning problems which take many years to resolve. Also, the school continued to function during the period of remodelling.

The sheer size of our stock of old school buildings inevitably leads to the conclusion that many of them will continue in use for a further ten or fifteen years.[1] The improvement of old school buildings in decaying urban areas is vital to the well-being of children reared in such areas, and this exercise has made a valuable contribution to the solution of a pressing social and educational problem, though whether it will be repeated on this scale appears very doubtful.

Conclusion In the post-war period, Britain has made large investments in school building and, year by year, there has been a steady flow of new primary and secondary school places, in spite of recurrent financial crises and fluctuations in the economy. For details of this, the reader should refer to Appendix I. The system of annual programming has ensured that building kept pace with both the increase and the shift of school population. Though over two-and-a-half million new primary places have been provided in England and Wales during this period, a good proportion of children still remain in old buildings. Capital allocations are now being made annually for the improvement of such buildings (£20 million in 1967/68).

Although the schools described here have been the subject of special studies in school building, they have all been carried out within the cost-per-place disciplines operating at the time of their erection. Such development work is publicized by the Department of Education and Science, local authorities and other bodies, as well as by the architectural and educational press, and essential

[1]The government recently (in 1971) announced its policy to improve primary school buildings erected prior to 1903, and substantial capital allocations are to be made annually for this purpose

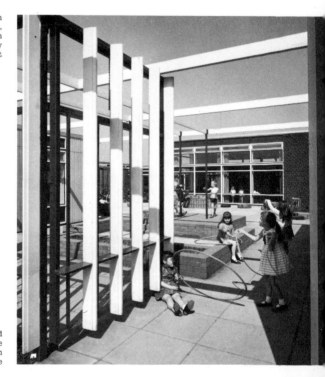

Frederick Harrison
Infants' School,
Stapleford; extension
of physical activity
to the central court

Typical industrialized
building by the
CLASP consortium in
Nottinghamshire

information is made available to all those engaged in school building. Innovation is not to be regarded as exceptional. Several local education authorities are applying, in their new primary schools, the standards and principles described in this booklet, and each year many schools similar to those illustrated here are built. The momentum grows.

A skilful architect will achieve both utility and grace in his building, however simple it may be. The designers of many of the Victorian and Edwardian elementary schools in England spent money on imposing exterior facades with ornamental cornices, gothic windows, stone dressings and wrought iron. Such manners have now largely disappeared from our new school buildings. While some people may regret this, others welcome the simpler, more honest buildings as particularly appropriate to a child's world.

How the work extends from a classroom to the area immediately outside

The extent to which these have resulted from choice or from the coercion of cost control will always be a matter for debate. Whatever the reasons, the resulting schools are gay, light, informal and ultimately domestic, and are fashioned carefully to the life and work of the children within. Thus, school building has not advanced merely on the basis of new building technologies or architectural manners, but on the needs of children as perceived by discerning educators and architects.

Appendix I

School building performance in England and Wales, 1946 to 1969

Year	New Schools		New places[1]	
	Primary	Secondary	Primary	Secondary
1946	—	—	20,000	14.040
1947	5	3	22,320	62,165
1948	15	13	37,765	96,890
1949	97	21	68,720	50,610
1950	191	48	89,280	38,360
1951	288	65	120,230	38,555
1952	439	49	156,620	46,765
1953	384	116	177,740	84,495
1954	436	160	125,015	72,035
1955	284	147	115,650	96,470
1956	225	214	107,595	130,575
1957	278	300	117,855	162,570
1958	221	375	98,080	196,830
1959	217	273	86,810	159,265
1960	225	187	83,305	133,525
1961	258	152	91,035	112,580
1962	269	130	81,490	112,880
1963	308	174	102,340	127,105
1964	393	187	116,250	161,970
1965	375	176	113,985	132,325
1966	429	106	162,100	105,460
1967	614	115	216,565	116,100
1968	736	101	254,225	110,510
1969	664	83	233,505	134,130

[1]New places are provided by the extension of existing schools as well as the building of new ones

Floor area of new building per school place

In recent years (1965–69) the national average for primary school building has stood at 40.5 square feet per place.

Appendix II

List of architects

1. Finmere Village Primary School, Oxfordshire
   Architects of the Department of Education and
   Science Development Group in association with
   the County Architect, Oxfordshire.

2. The Eveline Lowe Primary School, London.
   Architects of the Department of Education and
   Science Development Group in association with
   with the Chief Architect for the Inner London
   Education Authority.

3. Eynsham County Primary School, Oxfordshire
   The County Architect, Oxfordshire County
   Council, Oxford.

4. The Frederick Harrison Infants' School, Staple
   ford, Nottinghamshire.
   The County Architect, Nottinghamshire County
   Council, West Bridgford, Nottingham.

5. St Thomas of Canterbury RC Primary School
   Manchester.
   The Ellis/Williams Partnership, 1, Albert Hil
   Street, Manchester.

6. The Compton Primary School, London.
   Remodelled by Cassidy, Farrington, Dennys and
   Partners, 1, Mercer Street, London W.2.

Booklist

The following *Building Bulletins* published by the Department of Education and Science are available from Her Majesty's Stationery Office.

1. Relating particularly to primary school design:

No. 3 VILLAGE SCHOOLS (1955)
No. 16 JUNIOR SCHOOL, AMERSHAM (1958)
No. 21 REMODELLING OLD SCHOOLS (1963)
No. 23 PRIMARY SCHOOL PLANS (1964)
No. 36 EVELINE LOWE PRIMARY SCHOOL, LONDON (1966)

2. Of general interest:

No. 4 COST STUDY (SCHOOL BUILDINGS) (1957)
No. 9 COLOUR IN SCHOOL BUILDINGS (1962)
No. 19 THE STORY OF CLASP (1961) (The development of an industrialized system for school building)
No. 33 LIGHTING IN SCHOOLS (1967)
No. 38 STANDING AND REACHING (School furniture dimensions) (1967)

CHILDREN AND THEIR PRIMARY SCHOOLS (The Plowden Report), Her Majesty's Stationery Office 1967 (Chapter 28 *Primary School Buildings and Equipment*)

AN EDUCATIONAL BRIEF St Thomas of Canterbury RC Primary School. Published by the City of Manchester Education Authority

Her Majesty's Stationery Office publications are available in the USA from, Pendragon House Inc., 899 Broadway Avenue, Redwood City, California 94063

See also the following booklets in this series: AN INTRODUCTION, THE GOVERNMENT OF EDUCATION, SPACE, TIME AND GROUPING, A RURAL SCHOOL, ENVIRON-MENTAL STUDIES, A JUNIOR SCHOOL, FROM HOME TO SCHOOL, THE HEADTEACHER'S ROLE.

Glossary

For a fuller understanding of some terms that are briefly defined in the following list, the reader is referred to one or more books in this series.

Cooperative teaching
Team teaching. An example of cooperative teaching is described in detail in A RURAL SCHOOL.

Eleven plus (11+)
Term used to cover the procedures and techniques (eg, attainment and/or intelligence tests, and teachers' reports) used by local education authorities mainly to select pupils for grammar schools at the age of 11; formerly in universal use, now decreasingly, and only in areas where selection continues. A view of the eleven plus is given in AN INTRODUCTION by Joseph Featherstone.

Family grouping
See **Vertical grouping**.

Grammar school
Academic High School.

Half-term
Mid-semester (see also **Term**).

Hall
Multi-purpose space, large enough to hold the whole school (staff and pupils). Usually a large room, often combining the functions of dining hall, auditorium and gymnasium.

Headteacher
Principal. For an examination of the headteacher's work, and the differences between headteachers and US principals, see THE HEADTEACHER'S ROLE and THE GOVERNMENT OF EDUCATION.

Health visitor
Qualified nurse with special training who is employed by the local education authority to visit schools to check on the children's health.

Her Majesty's Inspector (HMI)
Her Majesty's Inspector of Schools. Appointed formally by the Privy Council to advise the Department of Education and Science, and schools, on the practices and standards of education; and to maintain liaison between the DES and local education authorities. See also THE GOVERNMENT OF EDUCATION.

Infant school	School or department for children from five seven or eight years old.
Integrated day	A school day in which children may pursue vario interests or themes, without regard to artifici divisions into time periods. The workings of integrated day are fully described in A RURAL SCHOO
Junior school	School for seven to eleven or twelve year olds.
Local education authority (LEA)	County or county borough council with responsi lity for public education in its area. See THE GOVER MENT OF EDUCATION.
Movement	An activity where the children explore expressi agile, and games-like situations. This is do through the dynamic use of the body, with spat orientation as it comes into contact with people a objects.
Primary school	School for children under twelve. It may be an **Inf school** or **Junior school** (*qq.v.*) or a combination of bo
School managers	Members of an appointed managing body of n fewer than six members who are representative various interests concerned with the school. Fo fuller explanation, and information on the pow and responsibilities of school managers, see T GOVERNMENT OF EDUCATION.
School year	This begins in September and consists of three ter (see **Terms**).
Special classes	Remedial classes.
Standards I-VIII	Grades in the former Elementary Schools (children from five to fourteen years).
Streaming	Tracking.
Teachers' centre	A centre set up by a local education authority provide opportunities for curriculum developme and associated in-service training for teachers. EDUCATING TEACHERS.
Term	The English school year is divided into three ter (cf semesters): Autumn (Fall), Spring, and Summ
Timetable	Schedule.
Tuition	Teaching. (In Britain, the word 'tuition' never the meaning, 'fees'.)
Vertical grouping	(also called **Family grouping**): Form of grouping, fo mainly in infant schools, in which the full age ra for which the school provides may be represente each class. See also SPACE, TIME AND GROUPING.

THE ANGLO-AMERICAN PRIMARY SCHOOL PROJECT
FORD FOUNDATION/THE SCHOOLS COUNCIL

INFORMAL SCHOOLS IN BRITAIN TODAY